EARLY LEARNING EXPERIENCES IN CREATIVE WRITING

by Imogene Forte and Joy MacKenzie

Incentive Publications, Inc.
Nashville, Tennessee

Illustrated by Gayle Seaberg Harvey

ISBN 0-86530-324-X

Copyright © 1996 by Incentive Publications, Inc., Nashville, TN. All rights reserved. No part of this publication may be reproduced, stored in a retrieval system, or transmitted in any form or by any means (electronic, mechanical, photocopying, recording, or otherwise) without written permission from Incentive Publications, Inc., with the exception below.

Pages labeled with the statement © 1996 by Incentive Publications, Inc., Nashville, TN are intended for reproduction. Permission is hereby granted to the purchaser of one copy of EARLY LEARNING EXPERIENCES IN CREATIVE WRITING to reproduce these pages in sufficient quantities for meeting the purchaser's own classroom needs.

PRINTED IN THE UNITED STATES OF AMERICA

Table Of Contents

ABOUT THIS BOOK 7
MAGIC LAMP 9
STIR UP A BATCH OF JAM 10–11
COLOR ME CRAZY 12
LINES THAT TALK 13
PUNCTUATION PILLOWS 14–15
SILLY RECIPES 16
HAND AND FINGER RHYMES 17
SOUND OFF 18
THE NAME GAME 19
ELF GARDEN 20
WORD POWER 21
WHEN I WAS YOUNG 22
FAME TO FRAME 23–25
CARTOON CONVERSATIONS 26–28
CHOOSE A LETTER—ADD A LINE 29
COUNTRY, POP, ROCK OR BOP 30
FUN "E" STORY 31
AUTOGRAPH, PLEASE! 32–33
WRITE A ROUND RIDDLE 34–35

TWO BY TWO	36
WORD PERFECT	37
TITLE TALES	38–39
RECORD-A-STORY	40–42
PULL-OUT POSTER FUN	43
TABLE FABLES	44
PING-PONG STORIES	45
CREATURE FEATURE	46–48
UNLOCKING SECRETS	49
INDIAN WRITING	50–51
THERE'S A SECRET IN MY CLOSET!	52–53
A PERFECT PET	54
A PUPPET PICNIC	55
WORDS FOR PICTURES	56–59
PICTURE THIS!	60–61
THE SOUNDS THEY MAKE	62–63
DISCOVER A STORY	64–65
THE W'S MAKE THE DIFFERENCE	66–67
A SUNDAE WITH SPRINKLES	68–69
ONE TO TEN WITH MY POETRY PEN	70–71
SIMILE CIRCUS	72–73
INSTEAD OF "SAID"	74
TEACHER NOTES	75–79

About This Book . . .

Early Learning Experiences in Creative Writing has been planned to help young children learn through experimentation, through creative involvement in directed activities, and finally, through the joy of discovery.

Young children are curious about and extremely sensitive to their environment. They instinctively push and pull, take apart and attempt to put together again, smell, taste, feel, and listen to things around them. "Why?" "What?" "When?" "Where?" and "How?" are words they use naturally and often. It is this interaction with their environment that parents and teachers can either nurture and encourage or inhibit and retard. Children who have had many happy, satisfying opportunities to use their hands, feet, eyes, ears, and whole bodies are much more apt to adjust happily and successfully to more structured learning experiences.

The purpose of the activities in *Early Learning Experiences in Creative Writing* is to help children understand and appreciate their environment, to develop self-awareness, to express themselves creatively, and to provide enjoyment and appreciation of literature.

The book includes a mix of simple hands-on activities, free-choice activities, and more structured teacher-directed activities. While instructions are directed to the child, an adult will, of course, need to read and interact with the child in the interpretation and completion of the activities. Ideally, the projects will be presented in a stress-free setting that will afford time for the child to question, explore, wonder, ponder, and create—and to develop an abiding, imaginatively inquisitive approach to creative self-expression. The fanciful illustrations will provide added incentive for lively interaction. Each activity is intended to contribute to the development of skills and concepts which will enhance the child's self-concept and serve as a guide to personal achievement.

MAGIC LAMP

Use wax crayons to color your very own magic lamp. Press hard as you color to make the surface of your lamp smooth and waxy.

Paste your lamp on a piece of tag or cardboard. Then carefully cut it out.

Make up some magic words. Shhh! These are secret words. Don't tell them to anyone!

Now rub your lamp softly and whisper the secret words. Pretend that a genie appears and grants you one wonderful wish. What would your wish be? Can you make up a story about your wish?

STIR UP A BATCH OF JAM

Stir up a batch of jam—story jam. Find three clean jars and cut out the pictures to fill each jar.

Pictures for Jar #1

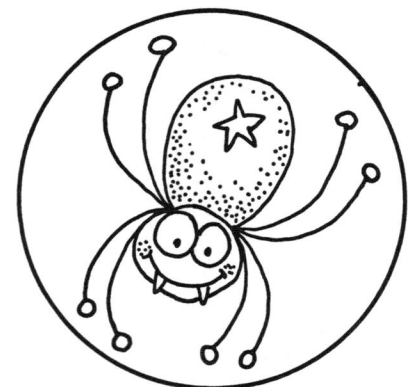

Pictures for Jar #2

Pictures for Jar #3

Close your eyes and choose one picture from each jar. See if you can compose a silly story using the three objects you have chosen. Ask someone to help you write your story or record it on a cassette tape.

© 1996 by Incentive Publications, Inc., Nashville, TN.

COLOR ME CRAZY

Choose a color for each big crayon pictured below. Then think of a word that you can use to make up a new name for each color you have chosen. For instance, you might color one crayon pink. Then you might add a word to make it a special kind of pink—such as Piggy Pink or Posey Pink or Kissy Pink or Bubblegum Pink. A brown crayon might become Teddy Bear Brown, and a white crayon may be called Ghost White.

Color both ends of each crayon a beautiful color. Then ask someone to help you write the new name you have chosen for each crayon in the blank space in the middle.

You may make many copies of this crayon and create lots and lots of your very own colors.

My Name Is _____

LINES THAT TALK

Smiley Line   Jaggedy Line   Twisty Line

Find a favorite pencil or crayon. Use it to help you make a special kind of line that matches each word below.

SHAKY

CURLY

FAT

WAVY

FLAT

KNOTTY

SKINNY

PRICKLY

Choose your favorite line. Make your line tell its own story of how it came to be.

My Name Is _____

PUNCTUATION PILLOWS

Use the patterns on page 15 to cut shapes of a period, a question mark and an exclamation mark. Cut two of each shape. Lightly glue a little pillow of cotton or polyester filling to one of each shape. Now cover each pillow with its matching shape and glue or staple the matching shapes together at the edges. Ask someone to read the sentences below. Listen carefully and hold up the punctuation mark that belongs at the end of each sentence.

Run, little mouse, run!
The mouse is cute.
Is the cat near by?

I have a new puppy.
Wow, can he ever bark!
Do you like puppies?
Puppies are a lot of trouble!

Never throw stones at animals!
Do you know any famous people?
Why are you smiling?
Don't laugh!
I am a funny clown.

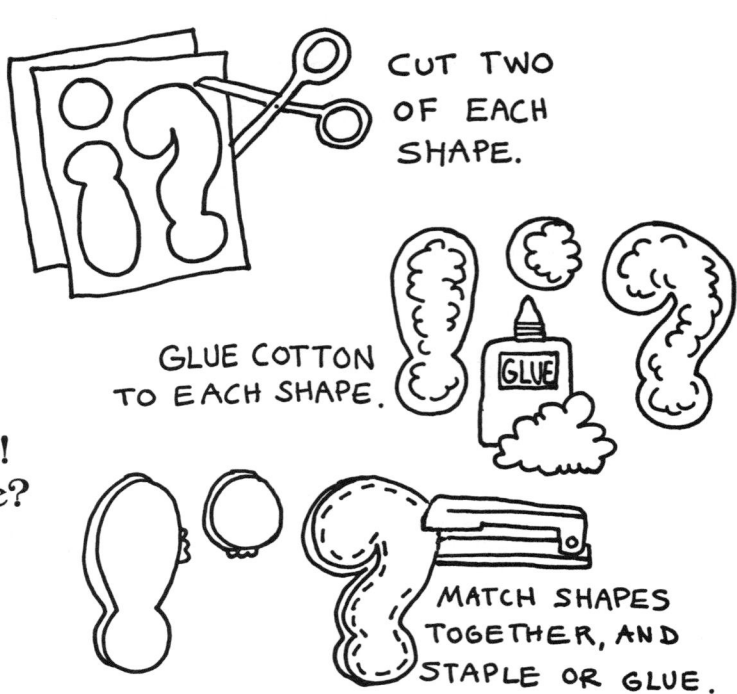

CUT TWO OF EACH SHAPE.

GLUE COTTON TO EACH SHAPE.

MATCH SHAPES TOGETHER, AND STAPLE OR GLUE.

© 1996 by Incentive Publications, Inc., Nashville, TN.

SILLY RECIPES

Make up a tasty recipe for hippopotamus soup or possum punch, tiger-tail tarts or kangaroo crunch.

Write your recipe in the special space below. Be sure to tell:
- how much of each ingredient to use
- how to prepare and mix them
- how to cook your recipe (IF it should be cooked)
- how to serve it

Use: T for tablespoon
t for teaspoon
C for cup

Add: a **pinch** of something
a **dash** of something
a **whiff** of something
a **speck** or squirt of something

My Name Is _____

16 © 1996 by Incentive Publications, Inc., Nashville, TN.

HAND AND FINGER RHYMES

Hold your hands, palms down; lock your thumbs together and use your fingers as eight spider legs to illustrate this poem:

Sneaky Spider

Tip-toe, tip-toe,
Tip-toe, tip-toe,
Spider sneaks across the floor.

Tip-toe, tip-toe,
Tip-toe, tip-toe,
Eight steps and he's there no more!

For the next poem, use the fingers on your right hand as the creeping mouse. Use your left hand and arm as the house. See how fast you can make mouse scurry to escape the cat!

Meow!

Creeping, creeping, creeping,
Comes the little mouse.
"MEOW!" He scurries quickly . . .
There's a cat in the house!

Can you make up a finger play of your own?

© 1996 by Incentive Publications, Inc., Nashville, TN.

SOUND OFF!

Think of at least two sounds made by each thing pictured. Then make up a new sound word of your own to fit each one.

  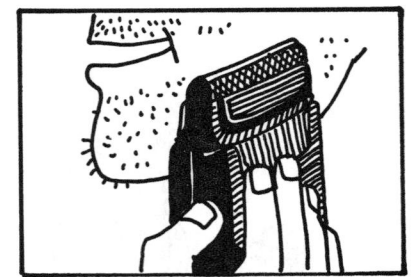

  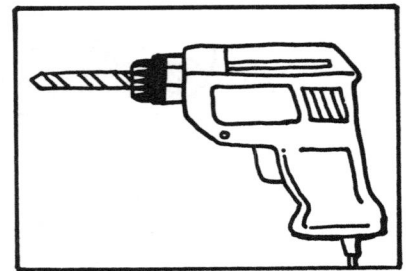

THE NAME GAME

Use your most imaginative ideas to make up a creative name for these silly new objects.
Write your new name in the space under each picture.

_____

_____   _____

My Name Is _____

ELF GARDEN

List all the things you might find in an elf garden. Use some of these things and your own imagination to create a tiny garden in a foil pie plate:

soil	moss	tiny plants	bark
seeds	pods	pebbles	a small mirror

Imagine that elves play hide and seek in your garden. Make up a rhyme the elves might sing. Spread a little sand on the ground near your garden and use a stick to write in the sand some of the favorite words from your rhyme.

WORD POWER

If you know how to use words, you have the wonderful power to change an idea very quickly. It often takes just one word! Read the sentences as they are written. Then change each idea by adding just one word to each sentence.

Example: I go to bed early.
I **never** go to bed early.

The boy saw a dog.   The little boy saw a big dog.

Add one word to change each sentence.

The boy saw a dog.

_____

The little boy saw a big dog.

_____

The scared little boy saw a big, grumpy dog.

_____

The grumpy little boy saw a big, scared dog.

_____

Make up a simple sentence of your own.
Then expand it by adding one word at a time.

My Name Is _____

WHEN I WAS YOUNG

When you were very young, your life was quite different than it is now. Think about how things have changed for you in just a few years. Then use the spaces to tell some of your story.

When I was young, I _____

_____,

but now I _____

_____.

When I was young, I _____

_____

_____,

but now I _____

_____

_____.

When I was young, I _____

_____

_____,

but now I _____

_____

_____.

My Name Is _____

FAME TO FRAME

Frame the writing of a future famous author—YOU!

Color these fancy frames, cut them carefully on the solid inside lines and choose a favorite piece of writing to display in each one.

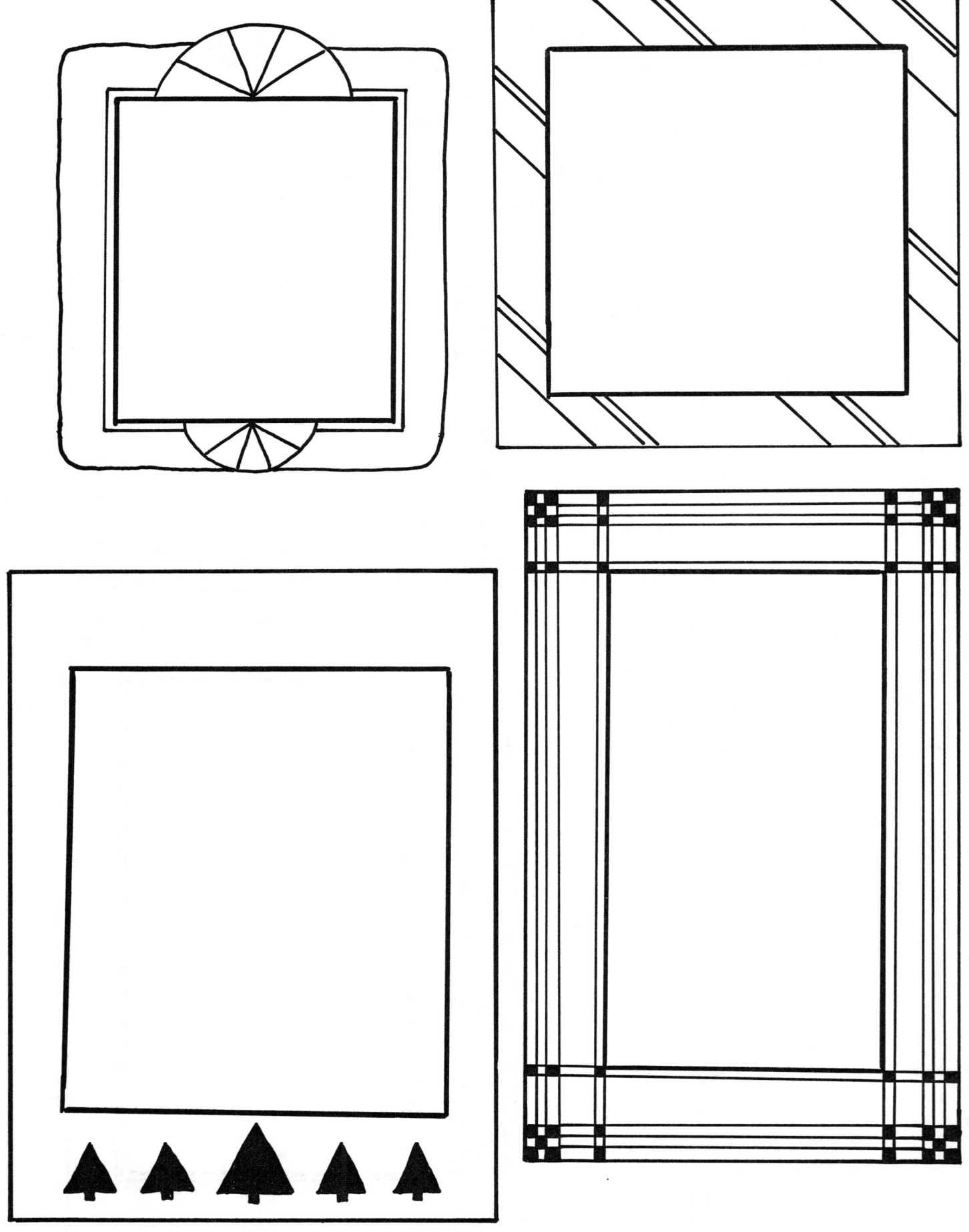

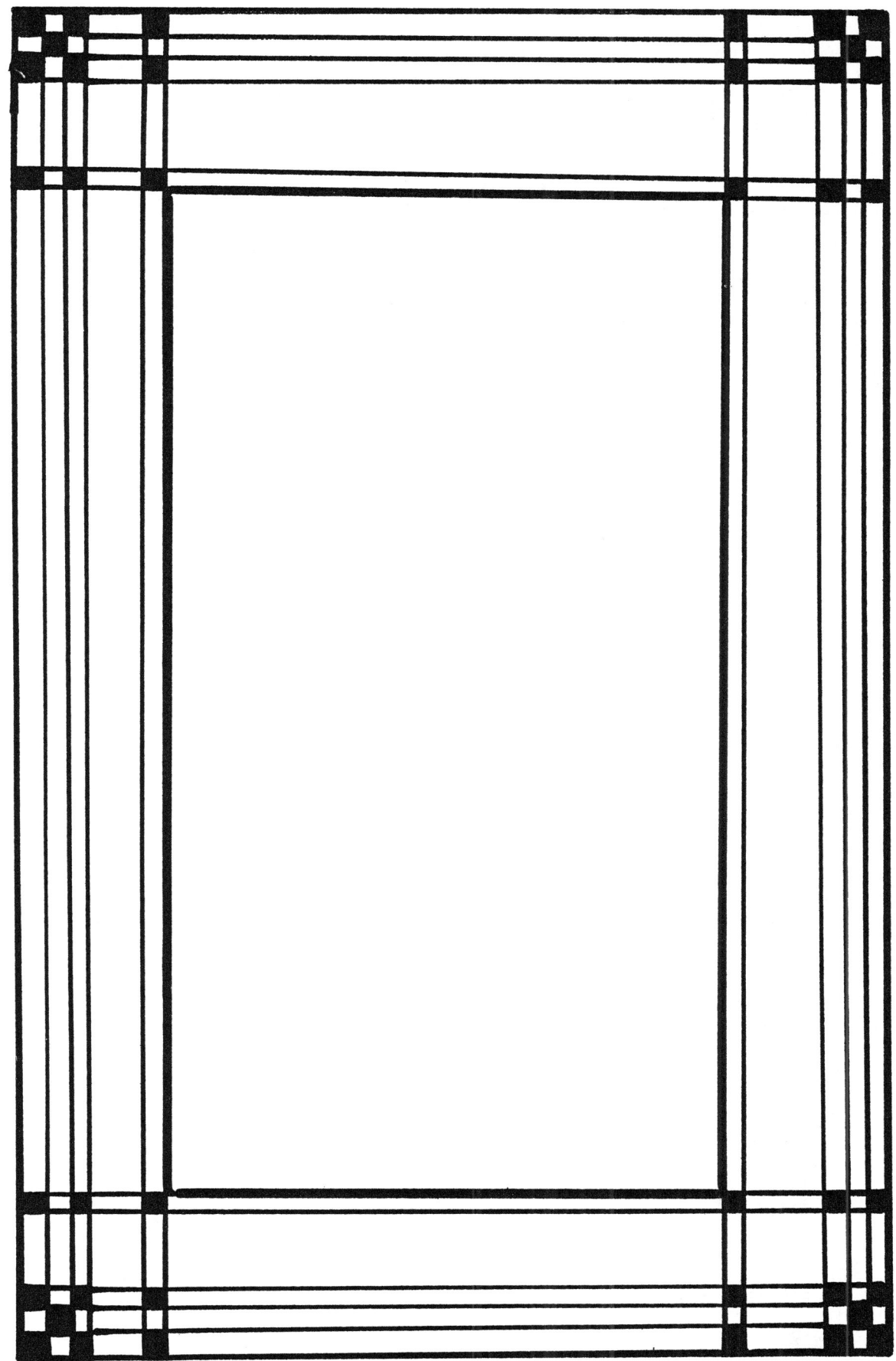

CARTOON CONVERSATIONS

Look at the cartoon pictures and decide what each participant might be saying or thinking. Write the words you have chosen for each character in the nearest talk balloon.

My Name Is _____

My Name Is _____

My Name Is _____

CHOOSE A LETTER —ADD A LINE

Cut on the solid lines to separate the letters at the bottom of the page. Place the letters in a jar. Have a pencil and paper ready.

Close your eyes and choose a letter from the jar. Look at the letter. You must make up a story about a person, place or thing whose name begins with the letter you have chosen.

This activity is fun to do with a friend or with two teams of classmates. Take turns choosing letters and adding sentences to your stories. See who can create the most interesting story.

When you have decided on the name, choose a second letter. Write a sentence that includes a word which begins with that letter. Continue choosing letters and writing sentences until you have completed a story.

© 1996 by Incentive Publications, Inc., Nashville, TN.

COUNTRY, POP, ROCK OR BOP

The wonderful thing about being a writer is that you can create many, many different kinds of things with words. You can write stories, poems, jokes, cartoons, letters, notes, plays, recipes, reports, riddles, speeches, ads, lists, bulletins, bumper stickers, and much, much more. Try your hand at writing something that can be set to music . . . a SONG!

To begin, choose a song you already know.
Hum the tune to yourself, and create new words to go with it.
Here are some songs that are easy to use:
Old MacDonald Had A Farm
She'll Be Comin' 'Round the Mountain
B-I-N-G-O
Skip To My Lou
The Twelve Days of Christmas
This Old Man
Here We Go 'Round the Mulberry Bush

Teach your new song to your friends and classmates.

FUN "E" STORY

The word bank will help you fill in the blank spaces to complete this "E" story.

WORD BANK: tree   bee   wee   knee
  see   me   three   flea   he

A w _ _ b _ _ came to s _ _ m _. H _ left his home in a tr _ _ to sit on my kn _ _ .

Along came a fl _ _ . Then there were thr _ _ — the b _ _ , the fl _ _ and m _ !

Color the picture of the three of us!

My Name Is _____

AUTOGRAPH, PLEASE!

Let's make an autograph booklet! Use the pattern to create a cover that is a face picture. Use scissors, crayons, yarn, buttons, glue, etc. to make both front and back of the head look a lot like you.

Draw around the pattern to make as many shapes as you wish for the inside pages of your booklet. Stack all the pages inside the cover. Fold and staple.

Ask each of your friends to write a special message in your book.

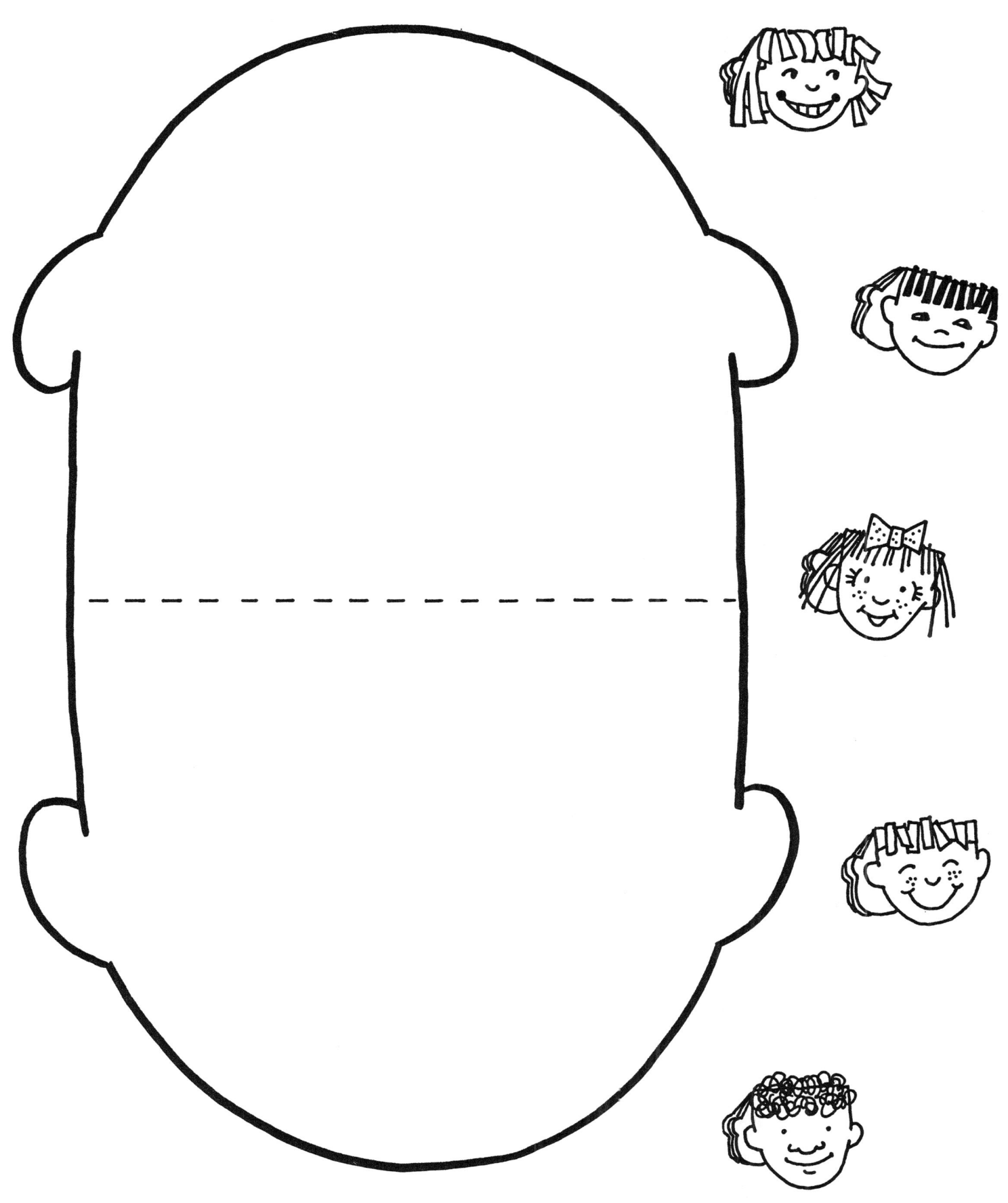

WRITE A ROUND RIDDLE

Why do birds fly south for the winter? To find the answer, follow these directions:

- In the #1 space, write the letter of the alphabet that means you when you are talking about yourself.

- In space #'s 6, 7 and 12, write a letter that looks like a donut.

- In space #'s 9 and 14, write the first letter of the alphabet.

- In space #4, write the letter that looks like a curly snake.

- In space #'s 2, 5 and 11, write the letter that appears nine times in this sentence.

- In space # 3, write an apostrophe.

- In space # 8, write the first letter of the name of the green animal that croaks, "Ribbit, ribbit."

- In space # 16, write the first letter of the name of the Australian animal who leaps about with babies in her pocket.

- In space # 10, write the last letter of something that twinkles in the sky at night.

- In space # 13, write the letter whose name rhymes with the words "trouble you."

- In space # 15, write the first letter of the word that describes what you do to an ice-cream cone.

Can you read your answer to the round riddle?

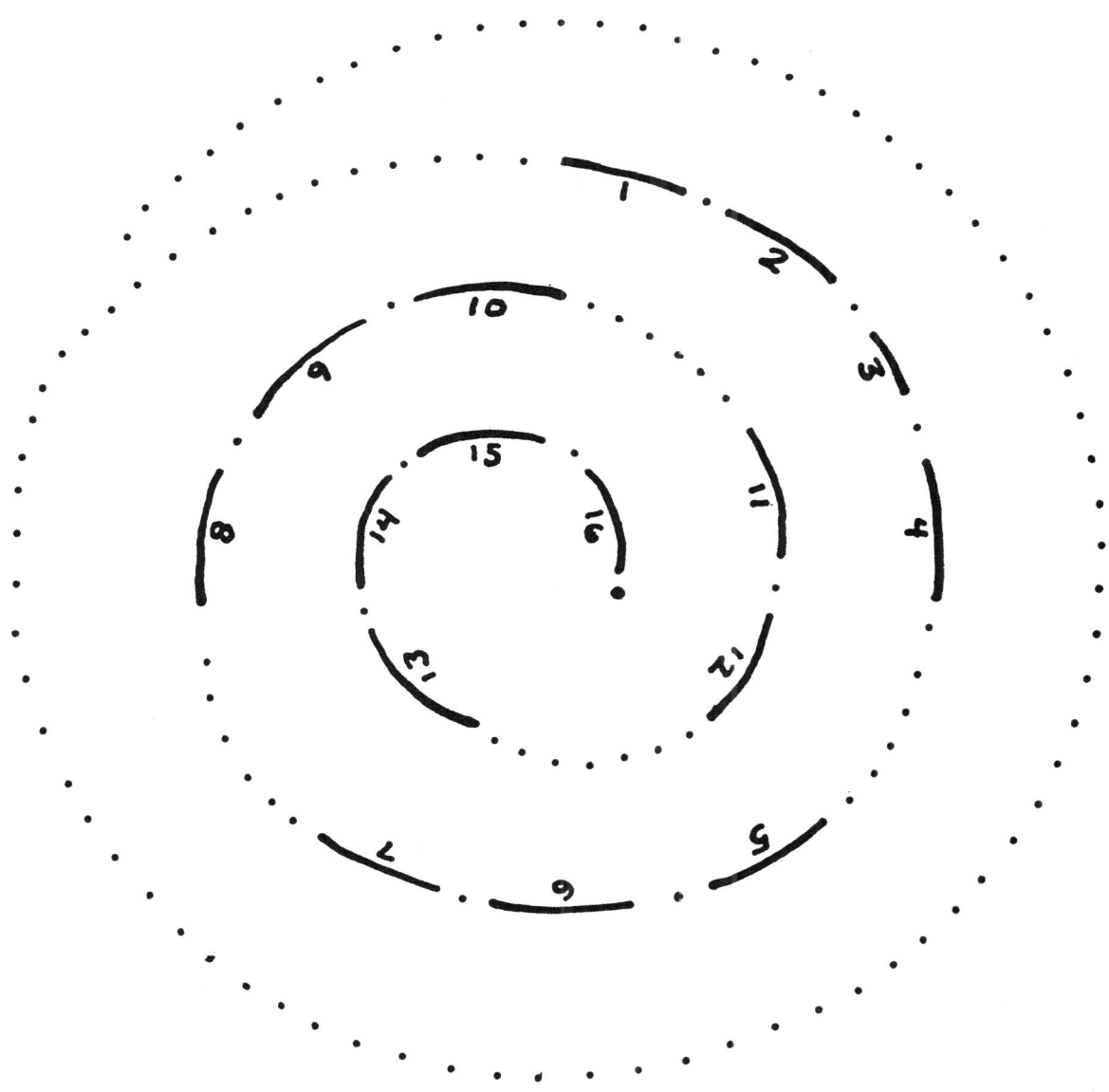

My Name Is _____

TWO BY TWO

A couplet is a poem of just two lines that go together nicely.
Usually the lines rhyme.
See if you can complete the second line of each couplet.

This is such a happy day.

_____

I'd like to live in outer space.

_____

Chocolate is super yummy.

_____

The turtle is so very slow.

_____

Please cover when you cough or sneeze.

_____

Congratulations! What a fine poet you are becoming!

My Name Is _____

WORD PERFECT

Color each picture. Then complete each sentence by choosing a perfect word to describe the picture.

1. This rabbit is _____ .

2. Did you ever see such a _____ fox?

3. What a _____ snake!

4. I just love this _____ flower!

5. Watch this bird _____ .

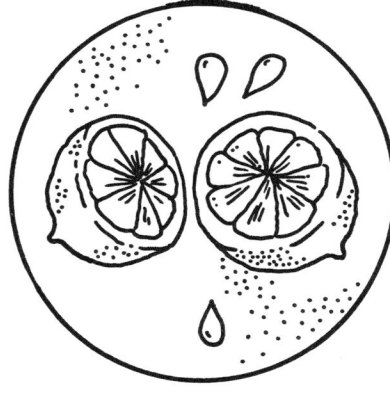

6. A good word for this lemon is _____ .

My Name Is _____

TITLE TALES

Create a good title for each book cover. Color the covers. The last space is waiting for you to create a cover all your own. When you have finished, make up a short story to fit one or more of your favorite titles. Write the story on the back of its cover.

My Name Is _____

RECORD-A-STORY

Choose one or more of the pictures on the following pages. Make up a story about the picture. Get ready to tell your story on a tape recording by thinking carefully about these things:
1. Who or what will my story be about?
2. What will happen in the story?
3. How will my story end?

When the tape starts, begin by completing these two sentences:

- This story is created and told by _____ .
  (your name)

- The story is about _____ .

Then begin to tell your story.

You may finish your recording with this closing sentence:

And that is my story about _____ .

OR you may make up your own closing sentence.

41

42

PULL-OUT POSTER FUN

Good writers are usually good readers. Find a few riddle or joke books to read. Then choose a favorite riddle or joke. Use a piece of poster paper and some colored construction paper to make a poster that illustrates your joke or riddle.

1. Cut a strip of paper.
2. At the beginning end of the strip, write PULL.
3. Then write the answer to your joke or riddle on the strip.
4. Staple a tab to the other end of your strip.
5. Cut a slit at the appropriate place on your drawing and slip the PULL part of the answer strip through the slit.
6. Share your poster with friends and classmates. Try to guess answers to one another's jokes.

TABLE FABLES

Read several fables or short stories that teach a lesson. Choose your favorite. Then create a "table fable" by following these directions:

1. Plan a series of pictures that tell the story.
2. Draw each picture on a separate piece of heavy tag or construction paper. (Be sure all the pages are the same size.)
3. At the bottom of each page, you may write words that go with that picture. (optional)
4. Arrange the pictures in sequential order.
5. Use clear tape to attach each picture to the page that comes before and after it.
6. Then turn the entire line of pictures over and tape the back side of each seam.
7. Fold the book like an accordion.
8. Set the book on a table or desk top and read it aloud.

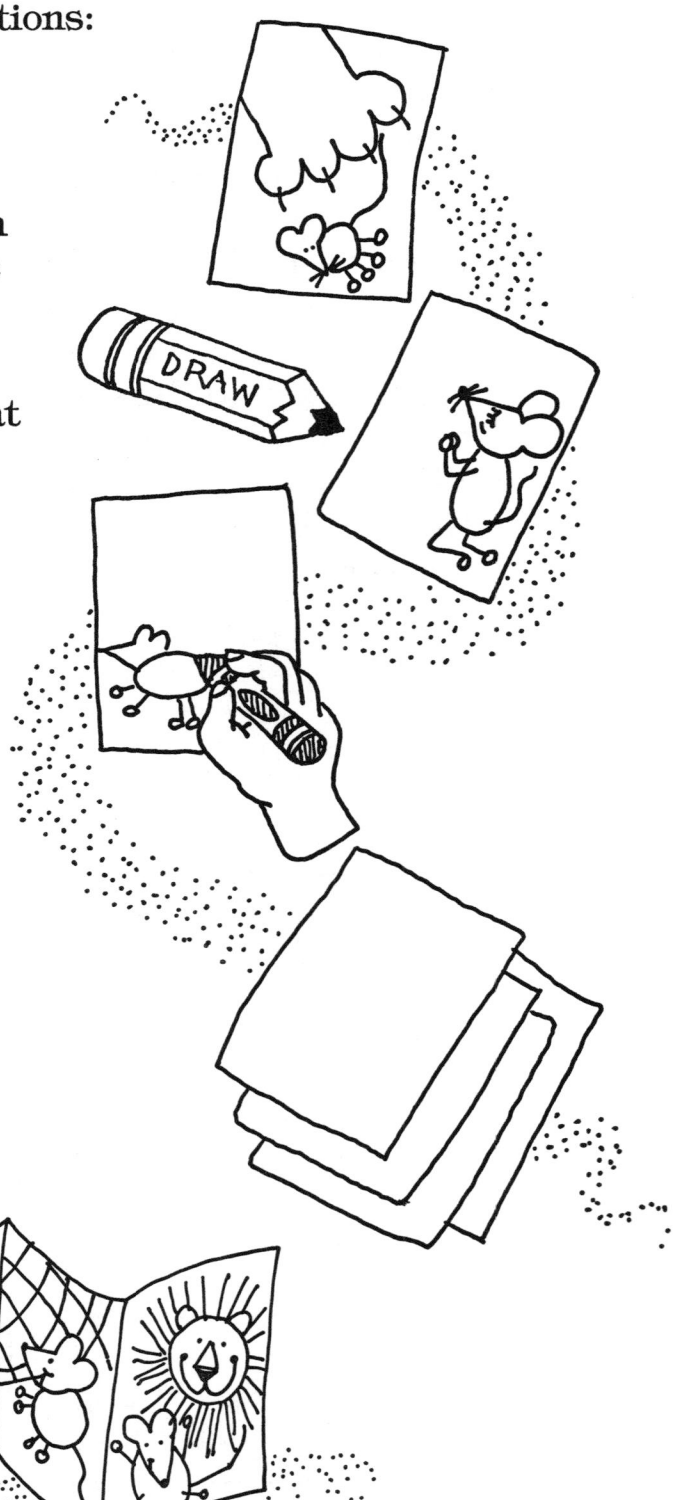

PING-PONG STORIES

In a game of ping-pong, the ball is bounced back and forth, back and forth between two players. Choose a partner and create a ping-pong story. One person makes up the first sentence. Then the second person makes up a second sentence. The first person adds a third sentence, and so on until the story is finished. Friends or classmates may watch the "ping-pong" game and enjoy the story.

Then perhaps some of them may begin a game of their own.

CREATURE FEATURE —A Story That Moves

1. Color the following story pages and creature shapes.

2. Cut and assemble the story pages. Look at the page numbers to keep them in order.

3. Staple the booklet together at the left edge.

4. Attach a small square of felt to the shaded box on each page and to the back of each creature shape.

5. Attach a plastic bag to the inside of the book cover to store the creature shapes when they are not in use.

6. Choose one creature shape. Make up your own story to go with the illustrations. As you read each page, move your creature and attach it to the felt square on that page. Then move the creature again as you turn each page.

7. Choose another creature and re-tell the story. See how different you can make the story this time!

⑦

MY FAVORITE
CREATURE STORY

— 1st Fold —

②

to _____

This book belongs

♡

Creature Feature

A STORY THAT MOVES

⑧

♡

①

UNLOCKING SECRETS

Think of all the kinds of things that keys can open: doors, boxes, vehicles, prisons, treasures, diaries, hearts, all kinds of hidden places—even secret plans and ideas.

Color and cut out your very own magic key above. On the back side of the key, write your special story. What will your key open? What will be hidden inside?

INDIAN WRITING

Early American Indians often wrote messages using symbols or pictures. See if you can use some of the symbols and pictures below to do some Indian writing of your own. You may mix words and pictures to make sentences. You may mix letters and pictures to make single words. You may also add pictures of your own. Write your messages on the next page.

🐝	Be, Bee
👁	I, eye
4	four, for
☀	Son, Sun
👃	knows, nose
🪚	saw
💍	ring
♡	love
R	are, our
↑	up
↓	down
🐜	ant, aunt
🥫	can
2	two, to
✋-h = and	
👑	king
💡	idea
🖊	write, right
O + 🔓 = open	

Can you read these messages?

My Name Is _____

THERE'S A SECRET IN MY CLOSET!

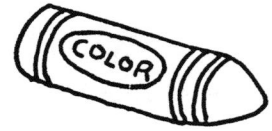

1. Color the picture and cut on the dotted lines to separate the picture from the page and make a door to your secret closet.

2. Turn your picture face down and put paste or glue around all four edges of the page.

3. Attach this picture to another piece of plain paper, using a pair of scissors to trim the edges so that the pages fit together exactly.

4. Think of something that might be hidden in a secret closet. It can be a special treasure or something very mysterious or scary.

5. Draw a small picture of your secret inside the closet door. Then close the door.

6. Now make up a story about the secret that is hiding in your closet. Don't tell what it is. When you finish your story, see if your listeners can guess the secret. Then surprise them by opening the closet door!

A PERFECT PET

Draw a circle around the animal that you would like for a pet. What are some reasons you would use to persuade your parents to let you have this pet in your home?

Write at least one reason on the lines below.

Color the pictures of the animals.

My Name Is _____

A Puppet Picnic

Color and cut out the puppets. Write a play about the puppets' picnic.

Glue a popsicle stick on the back to make your puppets.

Ask two friends to help you present your play.

WORDS FOR PICTURES

For each picture on these pages, make a list of at least three describing words, three action words and three places where action could happen. Ask someone to help you write your words in the lines beside each picture. Then use your lists of words to write a good sentence about each picture.

Describing Words
_____
_____
_____

Action Words and Phrases
_____
_____
_____

Places
_____
_____
_____

My Name Is _____

© 1996 by Incentive Publications, Inc., Nashville, TN.

Describing Words

_____
_____
_____

Action Words and Phrases

_____
_____
_____

Places

_____
_____

My Name Is _____

© 1996 by Incentive Publications, Inc, Nashville, TN.

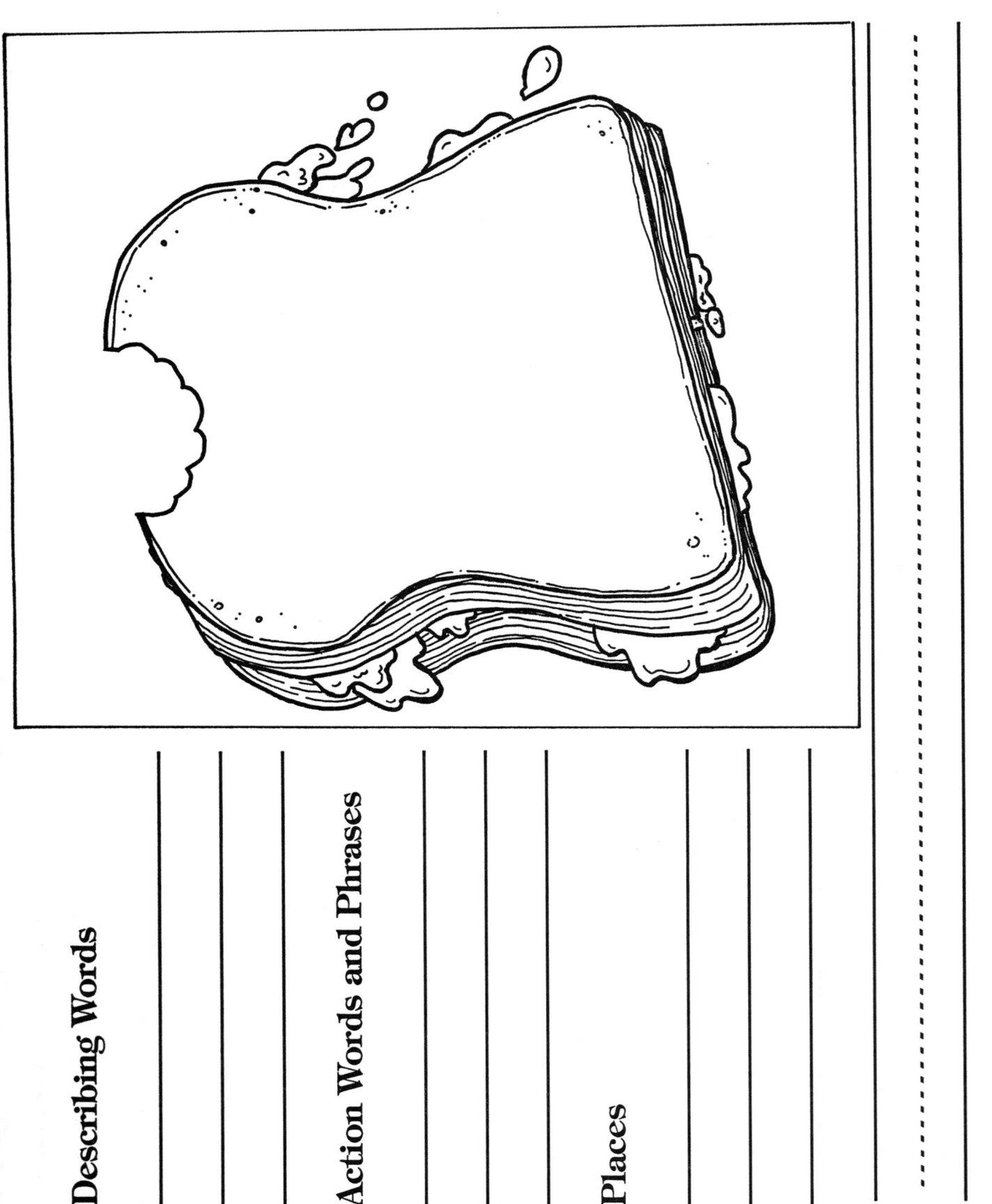

Describing Words

Action Words and Phrases

Places

My Name Is _____

© 1996 by Incentive Publications, Inc., Nashville, TN.

Describing Words

Action Words and Phrases

Places

My Name Is _____

© 1996 by Incentive Publications, Inc., Nashville, TN.

PICTURE THIS!

LOOK

Look carefully at the picture on the next page. What or whom do you see in the picture? Make a list of **naming words** that tell people or things you see.

Now look at the picture to see what each of these people or things on your list is doing. Make a list of **doing words**.

NAMING WORDS   DOING WORDS

_____   _____
_____   _____
_____   _____
_____   _____
_____   _____

On the lines below, write about at least one part of the picture. Use your lists of naming and doing words. See how many sentences you can write about the picture.

_____
······································
_____
······································
_____
······································
_____

My Name Is _____

60   © 1996 by Incentive Publications, Inc., Nashville, TN.

THE SOUNDS THEY MAKE

Ask someone to read each sentence below. See if you can fill the blank space with a good sound word.
At the bottom of the following page, draw a picture of your favorite sound. Write your sentence on the line below the picture.

   "_____" went the airplane.

Thunder _____.

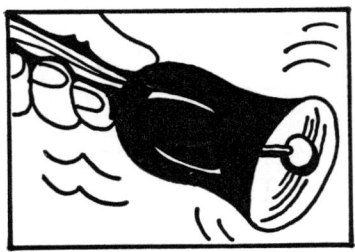   The school bell _____.

You can hear the waves _____.

   "_____" goes the wind.

Listen to the children _____.

   I heard its wings _____.

62

The brook _____.

"_____" go the scissors.

The bee _____.

The leaves _____ in the trees.

The bacon goes _____.

The old wagon _____ down the street.

_____
- -
_____

My Name Is _____

DISCOVER A STORY

Study these picture stories. See if you can discover for each story two letters that will complete all of the rhyming words that explain the picture. Fill in the two letters which will finish each story. Then color the pictures.

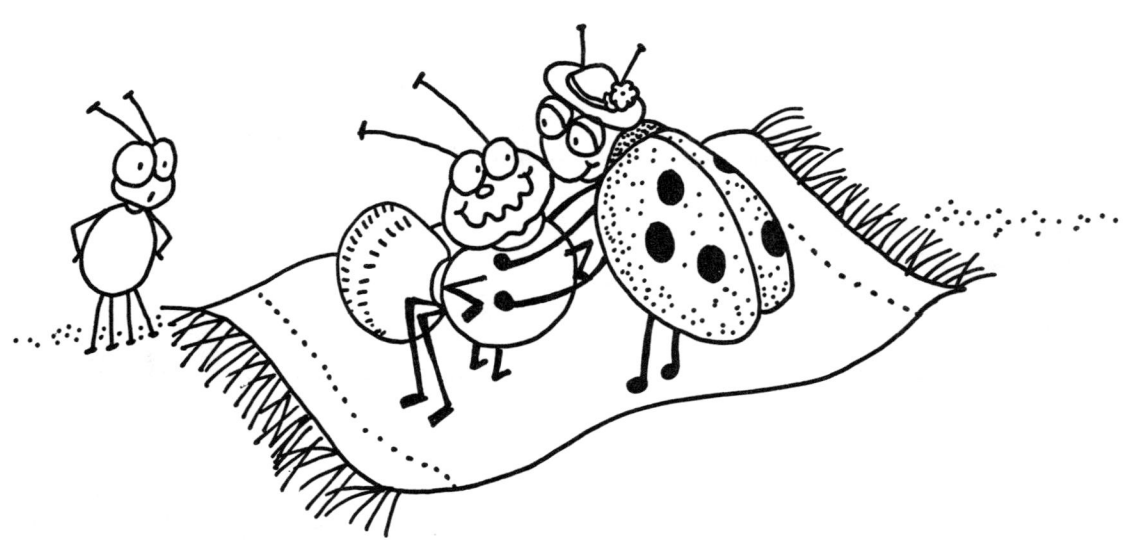

A b __ __ was sitting on a r __ __ when he felt a t __ __ . He turned to see a lady b __ __ who kissed him on the m __ __ and gave him a h __ __ .

A b __ __ p __ __ , wearing a funny w __ __ , ate a f __ __ and danced a j __ __ .

"St __ __!" yells the c __ __ as the burglar b __ __ s P __ __ on the t __ __ of his head with a m __ __.

"Thank you for the sandwich, Ma'__ __," said S __ __ to P __ __.
I love j __ __ on h __ __!

My Name Is _____

THE W's MAKE THE DIFFERENCE!

Study each picture carefully. Then answer the questions beside each picture. Use your answers to make up one or more sentences that tell a story about the picture. Write your sentences on the lines beside the picture.

Who? _____
_____

What? _____
_____

Who? _____
What? _____
Where? _____

66 © 1996 by Incentive Publications, Inc., Nashville, TN.

Who? _____
What? _____
When? _____
Where? _____

Who? _____
What? _____
When? _____
Where? _____

My Name Is _____

A SUNDAE WITH SPRINKLES

Find on the next page a delicious sundae with sprinkles on top. Yum! Yum! As you look at the sundae, think about all the ways it appeals to your senses.

Think of 5 words that you could use to tell someone how it looks.

Think of at least three words that tell how it smells.

Can you imagine how it would feel on your tongue?

How would it feel to stick your fingers right into the middle of it and stir and squish it?

Think about how your sundae would taste. Can you name a whole bunch of delicious words?

On the picture page, write some of the words you have mentioned.

Look for the part of the sundae that is labeled with each sense. Add some special words on each part.

On the lines at the bottom of the page, describe your favorite kind of sundae and list all the things you would put on top. Then color your sundae and add your own toppings!

_____

_____

_____

© 1996 by Incentive Publications, Inc., Nashville, TN.

My Name Is _____

ONE TO TEN WITH MY POETRY PEN

Beside each numeral on these pages, there is a box. In the box, write all the words you can think of that rhyme with the name of that number.

Ask a friend to help you make up a poem of two lines or more. You may use the sentence by each numeral as your first line, or you may make up a first line of your own.

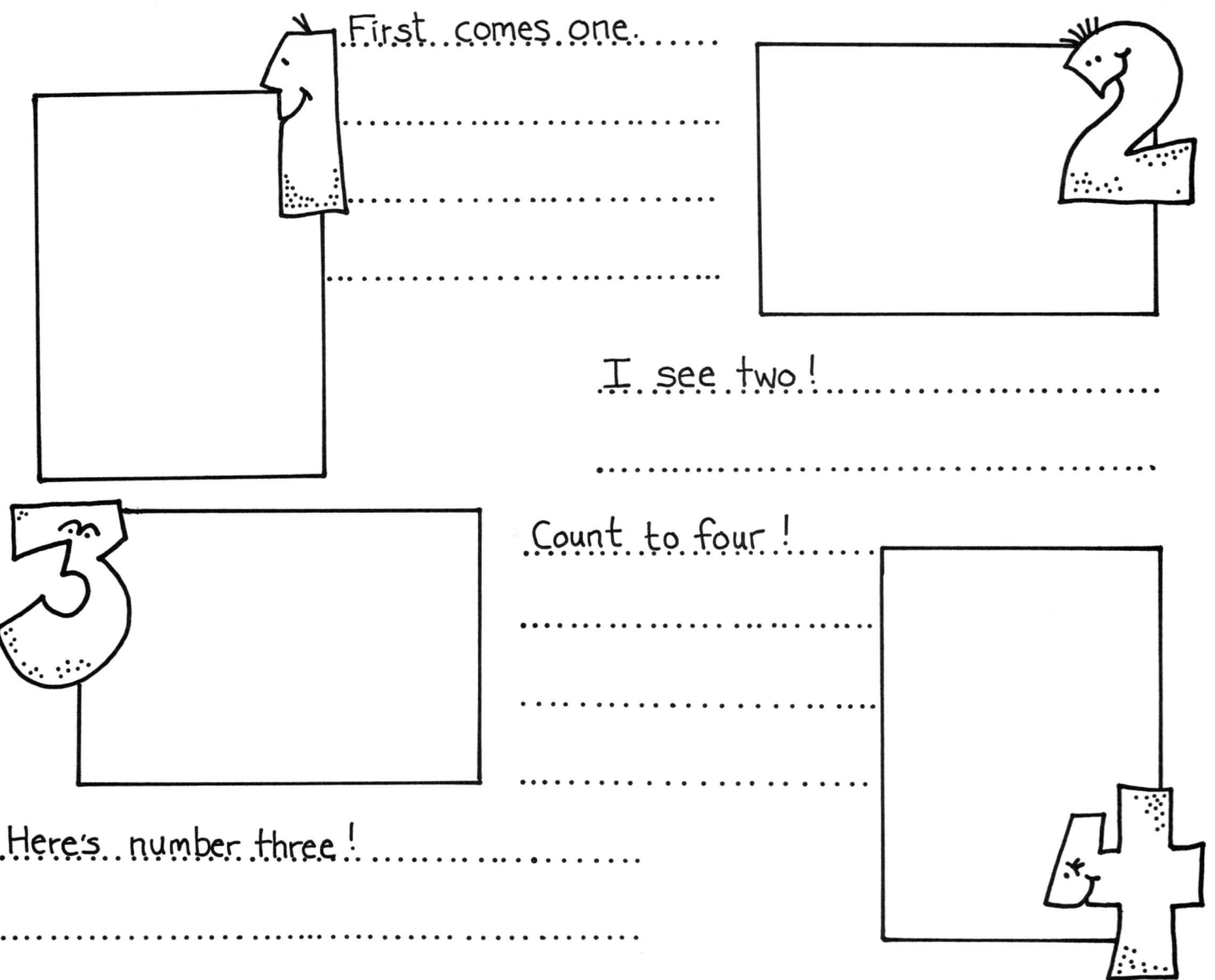

First comes one..........

I see two!..........

Count to four!..........

Here's number three!..........

A silly six ....
....
....
....

Hurray for five! ....
....
....

I like seven ....
....
....

Have an eight! ....
....

Can't beat nine ....
....

Last is ten ....
....

Share your best poems with your classmates or friends. See if, together, you can create a book of wonderful number poetry!

My Name Is _____

SIMILE CIRCUS

"A circus is like a big party." That sentence is a simile. It tells how one thing is the same as or reminds you of another thing. Look at the circus things pictured below. Can you think of something else that is like each one?
On the line under each item, see if you can complete a simile.

A lion's roar sounds like

_____.

Balloons remind me of

_____.

A clown's nose looks like

_____.

An elephant is big like a _____

The tall man reminds me of _____

The acrobats move like a _____.

Share your favorite similes with a friend. Ask the friend to choose the one he or she likes best.

My Name Is _____

INSTEAD OF "SAID"

When you are very scared, you don't **say** "Help." You **yell** "Help!"
When you stubbed your toe, you didn't **say** "Ouch." You **hollered** "Ouch!"
When Mom doesn't want noise to wake the baby, she doesn't **say** "Be quiet." She **whispers** "Be quiet."
There are lots of good substitutes for the words **say** and **said** that explain much better how the speaker feels when he or she is talking.

Think of a **better word** that tells how each figure below might say something.

My Name Is _____

Teacher Notes

From the very start, it is important to help young children view reading, writing, speaking, and listening as a continuously flowing series of language experiences. Optimum readiness for structured reading and writing activities is developed when the child views the printed page as just one more natural way to communicate with others, no more or no less complicated or important than speaking and listening.

Writing Projects

The abundant use of word cards, labels for familiar items, name tags, and other identifying signs and symbols helps establish writing as an important part of daily communication. A chart takes this concept one step further by focusing the child's attention on one specific and pertinent bit of information. Asking the child to dictate or contribute to a story or series of events to be printed on an experience chart for group use is a key step in preparing the child for independent self-expression. Structured pencil-and-paper activities requiring rigid adherence to rules and unrealistic assessment expectations can be highly detrimental to the building of interest in beginning creative writing projects, and can undermine confidence as well.

Writing projects that are outgrowths of the day's events make sense to young children and are non-threatening. This is especially true when the projects can be integrated into other learning tasks such as "picture book reading," science, math, social studies, and enrichment (art, music, drama, and movement). A few examples: writing the story a painting "tells," recording a step-by-step recipe for a treat, writing a puppet play, or writing a script for a shoebox TV presentation portraying the life of children in another country.

Greeting cards and notes and letters for family and friends, posters promoting a popular cause such as use of the library or conservation of natural resources, lists of rules for cooperative learning, and other communication methods provide good channels for early writing efforts. A simple way to keep your students writing is to create a post office or mailbox in the classroom with which students can communicate with one another. Use a simple box or paint a real mailbox and set it up in a classroom corner. When someone places a message in the mailbox, he or she raises the flag on the side and tapes to the flag a slip of paper showing the name of the intended receiver. Of course all messages must be signed and must be positive. When provided with word lists, examples of completed models, and adult guidance, young children will enjoy writing and sharing riddles, plays, rhymes, jokes, comics, personal experience stories, silly stories, lists, "how to" instructions, predictions, and other forms of creative writing.

Journal Writing

Keeping a personal journal for a designated period of time affords the young child a satisfying experience in both self-expression and increased awareness of the activities that make up his or her typical day. The complexity of journal writing activities is determined by the child's maturity level and mastery of skills and concepts.

The very young or immature child may use pictures and/or words in calendar squares to show a major event of each day (see page 77). The more mature child might be ready to use a collection of both or to construct simple sentences for a more typical journal approach. Other special journal writing experiences might include a field trip observation guide and summary, writing about personal holiday and special day activities, nature excursions, and reactions to special people, places, or events.

The Importance of Encouragement from Adults

As children begin to experiment with writing experiences, they seek and respond eagerly to encouragement and reinforcement from the adults in their lives. Parents' and teachers' attitudes strongly influence the child's interest in creative expression. Verbal praise, tangible rewards, and, most important of all, a sincere respect for the finished product are important components of the teacher-pupil relationship at this stage. Rewards need not be expensive or elaborate. The important thing is that they be meaningful to the child and that they lend themselves to showing, sharing, and displaying. They may take the form of certificates, ribbons, or simple on-the-spot notes. Other tangible awards might include teacher-made stickers, pencil toppers, doorknob hangers, or "bumper stickers" for chair backs.

See pages 78 and 79 to find ready-to-reproduce-and-use awards that can be prepared in advance to have ready for that magic moment when an opportunity for use presents itself.

My Week

By _____ date _____

☆ Monday

☆ Tuesday

☆ Wednesday

☆ Thursday

☆ Friday

© 1996 by Incentive Publications, Inc., Nashville, TN.